T
BLUFFE

CW00405759

MIDDLE AGE

ANTONY MASON

Oval Books

Published by Oval Books
335 Kennington Road
London SE11 4QE
United Kingdom

Telephone: +44 (0)20 7582 7123
Fax: +44 (0)20 7582 1022
E-mail: info@ovalbooks.com
Web site: www.ovalbooks.com

Copyright © Oval Projects 2004
All rights reserved, including the right
of reproduction in whole or in part
in any form.

Series Editor – Anne Tauté

Cover designer – Rob Oliver
Cover image – © Getty Images
Printer – Cox & Wyman Ltd.
Producer – Oval Projects Ltd.

The Bluffer's® Guides series is based
on an original idea by Peter Wolfe.

The Bluffer's Guide®, The Bluffer's Guides®,
Bluffer's®, and Bluff Your Way® are
Registered Trademarks.

ISBN-13: 978-1-903096-57-X
ISBN-10: 1-903096-57-X

CONTENTS

INTRODUCTION

For many, middle age is really no laughing matter. It's the point in life at which the end of youth must be declared and where the long, slow slide into decrepitude begins, heralded by birthday cards that declare: 'You know you're middle aged when... if you bend down to do up a shoe lace, you look around to see what else you can do while you're down there.'

Middle age is sometimes referred to as 'the sandwich phase'. Stuck between youth and old age, between adolescents on the one hand and ageing parents on the other, with pressure from above and below, there is an increasing awareness of the sell-by date.

This is where the bluffer steps in. Your task is to present the bright side of middle age, even if all the evidence to the contrary is staring you in the face — which of course happens to be one of the main sources of that evidence.

Middle age is a fertile arena for the bluffer's talents. And what makes it satisfyingly easy is the fact that, against all the evidence, most people in middle age are only too willing to believe there is a bright side.

Not long ago middle age officially began at 40 and ended at 55, though this was based on a perception of middle age derived from a time when anyone reaching 60 became a local tourist attraction. Today 40 is still in the full blush of fertile, child-bearing youth, and at 60 it's time to walk the Inca trail, throw oneself out of an aeroplane with a parachute, surf the wildest shores of the Internet, and road-test all those sex-shop products to destruction.

Middle age, the bluffer can confidently state, has taken an upward shift both in years and in status. But it lacks appropriate terminology. In line with today's go-getting upbeat attitudes towards the middle-aged, you might try using the term 'middle-ager'. This corresponds to the term 'teenager', which, after all, was introduced for the generation that is now pushing at the upper limits of middle age. 'Middle-ager' is of course a repulsive example of the way that the youth-driven modern world coins words with absolutely no respect for linguistic or etymological traditions – which is precisely why it is recommended. The bluffer does not wish to appear stuffy – or middle-aged.

DECLINE AND FALL

It can safely be asserted that at the age of 45 – even with the rapid advances of medical science – most men and women of the Western world are at least halfway through their lives. Somewhere around this halfway point, all of a sudden, it will dawn on a middle-ager that growing old is not something that only happens to one's parents, or to the cat, or to the old lady next door with her false teeth, her thick stockings and a house smelling of cupboards. In a moment of heart-stopping revelation, one day when waiting at the traffic lights, you realise this could happen to you.

And it could happen soon. At 45 years of age you may have got only, say, 30 years of good health to go, if you're lucky. Just 30 summer holidays left. Thirty springs with snowdrops. For the first time, your life span looks finite. Such intimations of mortality are so much a part of middle age as to be a defining characteristic.

A curious aspect of middle age is that the time horizon is now seen in terms of 30 years. For 20-year-olds, 30 years seems an interminably long time ahead. Fifty is ancient. Which of course is all wrong, as you must hastily assert. Nowadays 50 is young. Do not, however make this assertion in the presence of the genuinely young. They will never place 50-year-olds in any category that approaches young – unless they need money.

Bluffers know that a little knowledge goes a long way, but need to give a wide berth to the more famous downbeat references. For instance, Shakespeare's 'Seven Ages of Man'. He portrays the middle-aged as heading towards the pathetic, and eventually to 'mere oblivion, sans teeth, sans eyes, sans taste, sans everything.' We don't want that kind of talk.

The Forces of Gravity

Loss of youth is always a challenge, from the age of about 24 on. But when middle age arrives for real, it becomes clear that all those early worries about a bit of sag and flab were simply idle role-playing. That was just the pre-match warm-up. By the time the starting whistle has gone and the game is really on, the middle-aged are already shattered and looking forward to a hot bath. The mind may be willing but the body, it seems, has its own agenda. This process unfolds in two stages:

Stage One: It's not happening

The onset of middle age is signalled by a number of well-documented symptoms, and the victims have a stock of corresponding responses, which can be broadly summarised as a 'state of denial', e.g:

- You get out of breath when climbing the stairs (you always did, but you just didn't notice before).

- Crow's feet wrinkles appear at the corners of the eyes (the skin has simply adapted to your 'smile lines' and your happy disposition).

- You need to go to the loo in the middle of the night, every night (it's all that water one is endlessly encouraged to drink these days).

- A hairbrush fills with loose hairs (it's the moulting season which, thanks to El Niño, is now happening all year round).

Stage Two: Oh my God, it's happening

Bluffers should not allow the middle-aged to indulge in too much denial. Ultimately, if you deny that middle age entails inevitable physical decline, you might not address the symptoms before they get completely out of hand. Middle-age spread, for example, is a real and genuine phenomenon that has to be acknowledged. As Bob Hope succinctly put it: 'Middle age is when your age starts to show around your middle.'

Women are particularly sensitive to the relentless effect of gravity on flesh. Their breasts head south, their buttocks slide out of bathing-suit bottoms like overripe Brie, and their knees sag (but only in a manner that is perceptible to a woman). With high mileage on the clock, the body is essentially showing the first real, irreversible signs of wear and tear. In middle age, typical complaints are that:

a) teeth break when eating shepherd's pie;

b) hearing becomes less acute;

c) blemishes appear on the skin, not just moles but those tiny little wart-like things that cannot be pumiced away;

d) short/long vision declines and you have to guess the microwave times because the instructions are in micro-type;

e) because of (d) you become cack-handed and breakables get broken;

f) hair starts to thin and/or go grey;

g) the digestive tract begins working to rule, and stubbornly refuses to cope with peppers, bananas, boiled eggs and tequila sunrises;

h) serious injury to the lower back can be inflicted simply by doing two things at once, such as tying up a shoelace and sneezing.

The Grim Facts

The point that you need to make here is that all such phenomena – as demoralising as they may be – are entirely normal. As the body grows older, it loses its ability to maintain and replace cells. Human beings were not designed to ride into the sunset still sporting all the firm and pert attributes of youth. They were designed, rather, to fit the grand plan of furthering the human race through reproduction over the optimum years of youth, whereafter they are on borrowed time. They hang on in the post-reproductive age simply to pay the bills.

Eyes

By the age of 50, the human eye lets in 20% less light and the majority of middle-agers find it necessary to get spectacles for reading or close work.

The eye muscles, like the other muscles in the body,

get weaker with age, and the lens in the eye loses its flexibility, a condition called 'presbyopia'. Glancing up from a newspaper to the television seems like looking out at the room from the inside of a fish bowl; reading the programme unaided at a tennis match can render the ball invisible for the remainder of the game.

Presbyopia comes from the Greek, *presbus*, meaning 'old man' – but you don't have to rub it in.

Ears

The waning of hearing tends to be caused by the loss of flexibility in the eardrum and the three tiny bones (the 'ossicles') in the middle ear, or damage to the nerves that transmit information to the brain (e.g., by hi-fi at 100 decibels in one's teens). First higher pitches, then lower ones, become harder to perceive – which is why the middle-aged male appears to ignore his wife long before she starts to ignore him.

A study to measure ear length in hundreds of patients aged from 30 to 93 by British doctor James A. Heathcote and others, concluded that ears grow an average of 0.01 inches a year. In other words, ears grow larger as you get older. Of course you could claim that ear lobes increase in length with age because skin loses its elasticity and stretches, but it would be more impressive to propose that nature's response to receiving ever weaker signals is simply to enlarge the satellite dishes.

Teeth

The three main pitfalls with teeth in middle age are:

a) erosion of protective enamel;
b) discoloration (plaque forms more readily, and the

pigment in the bone-like dentin beneath the enamel yellows with age);

c) simple wear and tear caused by years of chomping and grinding.

Another problem is receding gums caused by the displacement of the gingiva (the soft tissue covering the bone supporting the teeth). The result is that more of the roots of the teeth are exposed, leaving the victim not only feeling but looking rather 'long in the tooth'.

Skin

There are several processes at work here. With age, the top layer of skin loses moisture more quickly and takes longer to renew. Young skin takes 3–4 weeks; old skin 4–6 weeks. To test this loss of performance, you can ask the middle-ager to pinch the fold of skin on a knuckle and see how long it takes to lie down again. Then compare and contrast with samples from other generations. It's a party game that will appeal to all generations, except the oldest present.

Since skin is the largest organ of the human body (the average person has 17 square feet of it including the bits beneath the hairy bits), in middle age wrinkles play an outsize role. A grasp of a few terms is bound to come in handy:

Free radicals. Although they sound like hippies riding naked across the desert on a Harley-Davidson hell-bent on reaching the anarchists' festival at Black Rock, free radicals are serious business. Also called oxidants, they are a single atom or group of atoms containing one or more electrons that is not paired with another. As they make a grab for electrons to pair up with, they can be highly reactive and damaging (like the singleton at a drinks party).

They are the loose cannons in atomic structure, found in flames and explosions. In the human body they damage cell membranes, genetic material, skin and just about anything associated with ageing in the kind of vague and mysterious way that bluffers are very comfortable with. They are Public Enemy Number One.

Antioxidants. These are the Good Guys, sworn enemies of free radicals. Over the years, through the pernicious work of free radicals, the skin loses its power to take up oxygen, causing wrinkling. Antioxidants, such as Vitamins A, C and E (known in the trade as the 'Big Three'), can help the skin to resurrect this process.

Lipids. Responsible for holding cells together, these troublesome oily components in the cell membranes harden and deteriorate in middle age, slowing down the process of skin renewal. The guardian angel of lipids is Vitamin E. The body's lipids can also be replaced by other light oils, such as ceramides, and linseed (also used to oil cricket bats).

Collagen. A fibrous scleroprotein (sclero- means tough, insoluble, stable, bungy) in connective tissue, collagen provides the healthy padded look of youthful skin, and, especially, the lips ('skinny lips' are a middle-age affliction). Troubleshooters are Vitamins A and C. Collagen can also be injected, and so is known as the 'plump-up' protein. If boiled, it produces gelatine.

Elastin. Another scleroprotein that gives elasticity to body tissue. Like knicker elastic, when slack it wrinkles.

Fibroblasts. Cells that synthethise collagen, and seem to have such a blast doing so, that after the age of about 40, they wear out.

Hair

Grey hair, thinning hair and baldness are critical issues in middle age, being the most obvious of all the signs of ageing. You may be able to offer some relief by relaying the fact that no-one – not even the medical hair experts, who go by the somewhat disturbing name of trichologists – know for certain why hair goes grey. It seems that the melanocytes responsible for imparting pigment at the top of the hair follicle simply take early retirement.

Grey hair is a mixture of white (in fact transparent) and dark hairs. In some lucky sods it looks silver, not grey, and rather distinguished. Be aware, however, that not everyone agrees with this upbeat assessment. Dating agencies have been known to refuse to take grey-haired women on to their books, deeming their prospects to be virtually nil unless they resort to truly convincing colorants.

A strand of hair grows more thickly the deeper the follicle. Thus as the skin thins with age, the follicles rise nearer to the surface and produce thinner hair. Or the hair just falls out completely. One of the holy grails of the pharmaceutical industry is a drug that can reverse baldness. Hopes have been placed in minoxidil. Originally developed to combat high blood-pressure, this has been found to stimulate hair growth and 15% of its users claim it to be successful. You could helpfully suggest to the remaining 85% that there is one other option: they can shave off all their hair and pretend that's how they want to look.

It could enliven a dull conversation to mention the close correlation between baldness and the continuing production of testosterone. The medical term for hair loss is alopecia; but in the company of the bald, it is wisest not to refer to baldness as a medical problem, and few would appreciate being told that the derivation of alopecia is the Greek word for fox. This is not a reference to the fox's reputation for being bright-eyed, cunning and a bit of a card, but to mange.

Digestion

The ability of the stomach and intestines to break down incoming food and extract the protein declines with age in line with the body's diminishing ability to produce gastric juices in the stomach, and the enzymes in the duodenum (the first 10 inches of the intestines) that perform that task. The result is the list of characteristic middle-age complaints, such as indigestion or heartburn and the inability to tolerate cheap wine – which makes a very good excuse to shell out on the more expensive kind.

The increase in semi-digested food in the intestines also results in a parallel increase in the production of gas. In middle age you find that carbohydrates, such as bread and pasta, as well as beans, onions, Brussels sprouts and red wine can become especially environmentally threatening.

Abdominal pain, indigestion and gas may also be the product of a medical condition known in the United States as TPS (Tight Pants Syndrome). It seems that many middle-aged men constrict their onboard recycling facilities because, when buying trousers, they tend to underestimate their girth by 3 inches.

Muscle and Bone

Bone cells are constantly lost and replaced throughout life, but in middle age a net deficit sets in, making them more brittle. Although it's nice to hear that more dynamic and exciting reasons are suspected, it is quite possible to put one's back out when simply

14

getting out of bed.

Muscle mass similarly drops away – by as much as 10% per decade for the committed couch potato. Meanwhile the joints dry out and cartilage erodes with wear. These are particularly dry after sleep, which is why going down the stairs first thing in the morning can sound like playing the marimba.

The Danger Zone

Those who in younger years complained regularly of mild medical ailments and were dismissed as a hypochondriac, in middle age will have the satisfaction of being taken seriously. Where once you were just walking around the periphery of the firing range, now you are walking right across it, and the weaponry is getting more serious by the day. As the years advance, so too does the incidence of diabetes, gout, gallstones, ulcers, arthritis, heart disease, cancer, and the inability to open the child-proof tops on the bottles of pills prescribed to counter all these ailments. Health failure becomes a genuine threat: those junk mail advertisements for private health insurance that went straight from letterbox to recycling bin may now be intercepted on the way.

The bald facts of the matter (an expression that bluffers should of course avoid) are that in middle age you cannot rely on your own body. It simply does not bend or mend as it used to. Health and good looks, so much a positive feature of youth, can no longer be so casually taken for granted.

The list of essential service-providers starts to include new groups of professionals such as chiropractors, osteopaths, chiropodists and proctologists (don't ask). Spouses will tell their other halves to take up a sport with an added sense of urgency.

Even that cautionary medical check-up can turn into a near-death experience, with the phrase 'pity you didn't come sooner' resounding around the surgery like a muffled drum. Having been read the riot act about high blood-pressure and cholesterol counts, it will be deemed virtually suicidal henceforth to put the salt on one's fish and chips – or to eat the chips. Living dangerously now means having a fried breakfast.

However, those who are feeling guilty for having avoided medical MOTs can be cheered by the information that their value is disputed. Some GPs complain that these cause unnecessary anxiety which in itself is detrimental. On the other hand if you wish to unsettle someone, offer the opposing view that severe medical conditions are usually easier to treat if caught before they have a chance to take up residence, and may be treatable simply by life-style changes rather than, after late diagnoses, by a life sentence of reliance on drugs.

In middle age, of course, the word 'drug' takes on a different meaning. Whereas previously it was associated with something obtained from a dealer which made the taker feel good, now it's obtained from a doctor and stops the taker feeling bad.

Exhorting the middle aged to abandon bad habits may well prolong their lives, but the mischievous might suggest that giving up 'life's little pleasures' could just make it seem longer.

Lapses and Delusions

'I've finally got my head together, and now my body is falling apart' is a familiar cry in mid life, so it seems unnecessarily cruel to point out that there is no guarantee that the head will stay in full working order either. The old joke goes: 'There are three signs

of age. One is loss of memory... I forget the other two.'
The term 'senior moment' has grown in currency to
refer to this age-related temporary lapse of memory.
Moments such as:

- forgetting your best friend's name when making
  introductions at a party;

- going all the way up to your bedroom and actually
  reaching for something before wondering what it
  was you came for;

- coming to the end of a long joke only to find that
  you can't remember the punch line;

- having difficulty remembering what you did yester-
  day, or ate for lunch today;

- looking everywhere for your spectacles when they
  are hanging around your neck.

Another term for this is a 'CRAFT moment': Can't
Remember a F...... Thing – which includes, conve-
niently, not being able to remember what the flaming
F stands for.

Loss of memory is disturbing – even if you don't
really suffer from it. What in youth was considered
rather charming, unworldly vagueness now looks like
the onset of senile dementia. Ever ready with reas-
surances, the bluffer will suggest that those suffering
from such lapses simply have too much to think
about. "Your brain is just full up," you will say with
conviction. This doesn't really help much but it may
allay the concern about it, at least until the next
lapse occurs – when you can safely repeat the line
because it, too, will have been forgotten.

The expression 'mild cognitive impairment' (MCI)
may come in handy. This is the technical term for the
condition that lies between 'normal memory loss' and

a more serious debility – i.e., the wheel is turning but the hamster is dead. MCI sounds comforting, and you don't need to point out that 'mild' cognitive impairment shares something with 'mild' cigarettes.

'Amnesia' also sounds faintly reassuring, like a cross between milk of magnesia and ambrosia. It just means 'forgetfulness', yet in a medical context can indicate a total loss of memory. A familiar condition of middle age is to be struck by amnesia and déjà-vu simultaneously, in which case you will have the uncomfortable feeling that you have forgotten the same thing before.

'Aphasia' (which sounds more like a girl's name than a problem) is the rather more serious condition of partial or total loss of the ability to communicate (through a disorder of the central nervous system, but you needn't go that far). A mild form of this occurs frequently in middle age, manifesting itself in the inability to remember where one was headed with a sentence, or finding that you cannot quite access a perfectly simple word in the sentence – usually the one that counts.

The Brain

Brain research reveals that as time goes by:

- There is a net decrease in brain-cells. (But you can point out that since average 70-year-olds still have 90% of the brain cells they had at 25, in middle age one can afford to lose a few.)

- Neurons (cells conducting the nerve impulses) become less efficient, slowing down the brain's work rate, so mental speed – how quickly the mind reacts (e.g., driving) – decelerates and starts fiddling with the glove compartment.

18

- The frontal lobes, home to the brain's 'working memory' that deals with current tasks (as opposed to memories of childhood), are affected, which explains why once you reach middle age your desk gets covered in post-it notes to yourself.

- The ability to learn is impeded by deterioration of the temporal lobes, that part of the brain which is assigned the task. This, you can blithely assert, is probably at the root of the old adage: 'you can't teach an old dog new tricks.'

Fortunately, there are some positive straws to clutch on to. Research suggests that, although most of the body stops growing in early adulthood, the brain actually continues to grow into middle age. This may account for those attributes that accrue in middle age such as wisdom and emotional stability – even if only because you've forgotten whatever it was that was making you emotionally unstable.

In fact, some neurologists insist that mental ability does not necessarily decline with age at all, and the removal of surplus and redundant brain cells can actually bring benefits, like clearing the garage of old paint pots. Tests have proven that, if kept mentally active, older people can outperform younger competitors – and that isn't just being able to sing all the words to songs by Leonard Cohen. At the Open University the best results are achieved by 60–65 year-olds.

Should your audience be known to recoil from anything so demanding as learning, try approaching from the other end, and advocate going barefoot. Californian doctor John Douglas claims this is not only good for the feet, but may also protect against decrepitude by stimulating the grey matter (brain not hair), since you have to concentrate on where you put your feet. 'To the best of my knowledge,' he states, 'people who go barefooted have little memory loss.'

'The only drawback to this,' you will say ruefully, 'is coming face to face with your feet, which will make you wonder what on earth you did to them to get them looking like that.'

Self-Deception

Middle age above all is a time for self-deception. The middle-aged are adept at believing what they want to believe and at screening out what they do not wish to see and hear. For instance, you feel you are younger than you are. Every now and then, when you are brought up short by brutal reality, self-deception soon takes over, for example:

- You walk naked into a hotel bathroom and catch sight of a worn-out, overweight stranger in the bathroom mirror – before realising that it's you. (Excuse: badly made mirrors.)

- A holiday snap reveals you with brutal honesty. (Excuse: cameras have an unfailing knack of catching you in an unrepresentative pose.)

- When watching television, a tiny tot runs to the screen, points to an ageing, worn-out, plug-ugly character and shouts your name. (Excuse: television overstimulates the young mind.)

A similar mechanism appears to shield the middle-aged from the fact that ageing amplifies their ingrained bad habits and defects – facial tics, nervous throat-clearing, inappropriate surges of enthusiasm, delusions about being an irresistible sex symbol, drinking everything in sight.

Signalled in youth, when they were forgiven with a shrug, in middle age these idiosyncrasies are blown up on to a wide screen. Under the effect of alcohol, middle-agers tend to repeat themselves in conversation, returning to the same old stories time and again; and they start to recognise true friends in those who try to prevent them from doing so – provided the friends can remember the stories in the first place, or are sober enough to care.

The Flight of the Hormones

Also beating a retreat in middle age are the hormones, and most famously the sex hormones. This, you will point out, is of course all part of the grand plan. In theory, procreation takes place in youth. That done, the sex hormones are no longer required. The result is mayhem, as the body says goodbye to these companions of youth and tries to cope without them.

Menopause

The decline of oestrogen in women is far more dramatic than the loss of testosterone in men. During the menopause, women lose 95% of their oestrogen. The result is: permanent exhaustion, loss of concentration, wild mood swings (between weepiness, irritability and explosions of gunfire-grade anger); reduced libido; vulnerability to osteoporosis; night sweats, heat surges, and chin hair which, because of failing eyesight, the victims can't see to remove.

Though the mechanisms involved in the menopause remain something of mystery, it is enough to assert that the loss of oestrogen affects every aspect of the body: the central nervous system, the brain, the bones. For instance, the hot flushes (more excitingly called 'flashes' in the U.S. which suggest a sudden brainwave) are thought to be caused by the way that the loss of oestrogen affects the brain's chemicals and the neurotransmitters that control body temperature. Serotonin, a neuro-whatsit associated with mood, is similarly affected.

No-one knows quite why the female body suddenly abandons fertility (at the average age of 51), and what function this genetically inherited switch serves. The theory is that the human family found it worthwhile having grannies around to dish out wisdom and solace when their own daughters started producing babies, without complicating matters by continuing to produce offspring of their own.

Happily, the end of fertility has its blessings, as long as it is treated it with the mistrust normally reserved for card sharks. Otherwise couples may find themselves, after a nostalgic night of passion, victims of (or 'blessed by', depending on who you are talking to) the 'late baby' phenomenon.

Even the run-up to the menopause – the 'peri-menopause' – can be something of a rollercoaster ride. In a farewell gesture, fertility – behaving like the Joker in *Batman* – is capable of producing some curious effects in women, such as a sudden desire to have children when they never wanted any before; an unquenchable need for oral gratification (lipstick, chocolate, cigarettes); plus a supercharged surge in sex drive. In this condition women, in brief, suddenly may find themselves behaving rather like men.

Andropause

It is suggested that men go through an ageing watershed similar to that of women – a phenomenon called the 'andropause' or 'viropause or 'male menopause' – take your pick. The concept has been around since it was first singled out in 1975 by Raymond Hull and Dr. Helmut J. Ruebsaat. Medical science is still resistant to the idea, but numerous symptoms are identified – all of them less obvious and severe than their female equivalents.

Menopausal men become more fatigued, bored, depressed, moody and peevish. They can wake up in the middle of the night and, racked by vague anxieties, cannot go back to sleep. Some even have hot flushes. Joints become stiff, skin becomes dry. Meanwhile, they are also balding, putting on a paunch, developing 'man-breasts', doubling their chins, and sprouting rank tufts of curiously wiry hair from their noses and ears.

At the same time they may suffer from a loss of sex-drive and impotence – or just the worry of it. According to the experts, erectile dysfunction is a problem that affects 50% of men aged between 40 and 70. This is the sort of vague statistic the bluffer can bandy about with confidence, knowing that it is virtually impossible to test (men are notoriously cagey about such things, and why would women tell?).

The gradual reduction of the sex hormone, testosterone, is the culprit; it declines by 50% between the ages of 25 and 75. At the age of 50, about half of all men – and that's not just the lower half – will have lost sufficient testosterone to reduce their sex drive to a level well below that of their youth. Blame for this can apparently be laid at the door of the SHBG ('sex hormone binding globulin'), which in middle age rolls around the body picking up loose testosterone like a ball of Blu-Tack in a drawer.

The most obvious symptom of the male menopause is the transparent effort to compensate for a general decline in mid-life performance. This is manifested in the vain effort to recapture the lost thrills of youth, and may explain the attraction to many menopausal men of high-risk pursuits, such as hang-gliding, kendo, flamenco-dancing, and wearing spandex shorts.

The classic manifestation of this stage in men's middle age is the desire to go out and buy the dream sports car of their youth (the 'menoporsche'), before it really is too late. The result is often ludicrous – the reverse equivalent of the adolescent who thinks he looks old by smoking a cigarette.

A more drastic but well-tested option is to trade in their wives for a younger model. If you are the forgiving kind (or bluffing people not remotely connected to those involved), you might like to push the theory that this is the product of the genetic imperative to procreate: the fertility of the male has outlasted the fertility of a female partner of the same age and simply needs somewhere else to go. Genetic imperative is the one area of life over which men are happy to claim they have no control.

Hormone Replacement

The theory of hormone replacement has the appeal of simplicity. If the discomforts of the menopause and the andropause are caused by the loss of hormones, then the answer lies in replacing them.

Women were the first beneficiaries. In the 1960s HRT was introduced to help sufferers of very severe symptoms of the menopause – notably fatigue, loss of concentration, and a wonky thermostat. The bouncy rejuvenation and prolongation of sex drive that it induced in many users aroused the envy of others, so HRT has now become an option and, despite widely publicised downsides, is described by many in such terms as 'a new lease of life'.

Much more mileage can be had by discussion of natural alternatives to HRT, such as acupuncture, homeopathy, and plant-based phyto-oestrogens (as found in soya products, wild yams and linseed oil), supported by more exercise (for those brittle bones), a change in diet, and Vitamin B supplements. A soya-enriched loaf of bread specifically targeted at women seeking relief from menopausal symptoms is now selling at a quarter of a million loaves per week – and rising.

Meanwhile, the pharmaceutical industry – never known to miss a trick – has decided the andropause is a medical problem that can be treated with TRT (Testosterone Replacement Therapy). Furthermore, it is claimed that, as well as benefiting men, TRT can also benefit women. Testosterone occurs naturally in both sexes, and it appears that a post-menopausal woman who takes a testosterone supplement can revive a flagging libido and even match the increased vigour of her TRT-powered partner – without getting a hairy chest.

Should you find yourself bluffing in the run-up to Christmas, suggest joint TRT treatment as a his 'n hers present.

First Aid

Bluffers will be sore pressed to counter such a deluge of irrefutable evidence of advancing physical and mental decline in middle age. But a good way to start is by reminding the afflicted middle-ager that in fact he or she is still young, comparatively speaking.

Suggest that in middle age, many people (you may have to speak in broad terms, depending on the case) still have their looks/health/vigour (delete as necessary) – but in addition they have the experience of age to put these assets to best use, as never before.

Adapt the truism 'Youth is wasted on the young'. In another 20 years' time, middle-agers do not want to look back on their middle-age years and see them as wasted youth. (They've done that once already.)

Few people tire of hearing Victor Hugo's assertion 'Forty is the old age of youth, fifty is the youth of old age.' You can ram it home by saying that old age may seem like a long way off, but on the day it doesn't, it will be too late to do anything about it. And while this is still sinking in, switch the conversation to a non-age-related topic, if you can find one.

GRUMPY, CRUSTY, CRABBY

Growing older can be felt not only in terms of physical and mental deterioration, but also in attitudes. The person who in youth was labelled an uncompromising idealist and rebel will in middle age be criticised as an old curmudgeon – even if expressing the same views.

According to received wisdom, as one gets older one becomes more conservative, grumpy, predictable and risk-averse. Crabby, crusty habits and attitudes harden. If you were once set in your ways you are now in a rut, if not deeply entrenched. You want your meals at specific times. You loathe drinking tea out of any cup that isn't bone china, or wine from a plastic beaker. You cling to your views as tenaciously as a corn plaster.

Blaming the Young

The middle-aged are often accused of relentlessly criticising youth. Yet it seems this is a time-honoured and inescapable symptom of ageing. Dr. Johnson recognised it in the 18th century: 'Every old man complains of the growing depravity of the world, of the petulance and insolence of the rising generation.'

Since it is the bluffer's task to make middle age sound good, you could bring up the benefits to mental health of sounding off. It stimulates the mind and body. As the American writer Logan Pearsall Smith put it: 'The denunciation of the young is a necessary part of the hygiene of older people, and greatly assists the circulation of the blood.'

The middle-aged complain about the young and may envy them, but few would actually want to be young again. So you can confidently quote Asquith's assertion that: 'Youth would be an ideal state if it came a little later in life.'

How to Spot the Types

The middle aged, you will insist, are far from uniform and can be divided into at least five categories, not all of which are set in their ways like cement:

1. Young after their time

Forever buoyant, forever relishing new and exciting ideas, these are the friends who will keep their peer group in touch with what's new in the world – in pop music, television and patterns for pubic hair waxing. They will dress beneath their age and weight, and draw attention to themselves in public places.

Critics will call them desperate, but they perform admirable service as a bridge between the young and the old. The young, once they have got over the embarrassment, appreciate having people older who seem to want to listen to them. The old, though disconcerted by their calculatedly unconventional social habits, warm to them because they transmit the vital essence of youth, which can be taken intravenously.

2. **Old before their time**
These middle-agers tend to model themselves on their parents, in clothing, hairstyle and attitudes. They are bored with their dead-end jobs, and just can't wait to get out their slippers and quietly go to seed. They detest anything that smacks of youth culture, and nothing in their entire world gives them greater pleasure than having their prejudices confirmed. They are convinced that things will only get worse. Advise your audience not to criticise those who are old before their time: they are solid citizens and the backbone of society, which is always thankful to have them when things go wrong.

3. **Stuck in time**
From the hippy bangles to the ponytail, there are tell-tale signs for those who are living in a bubble of the past, studiously mothballed in the era when they were happiest, the era that defined them. They are not necessarily critical of the modern world; in fact, they believe they are very much part of it. They even have mini-disc players and iPods and can download MP3s – usually digitally remastered versions of their favourite tracks from the vinyl years.

4. **Doing time**
With this category it is easier just to tick the boxes. They have dependable jobs, a house and mortgage, school-age children, a limited circle of friends, an interest in sport, and a Sunday-newspaper knowledge of the world. Life is fine. But there is always rather too much to do, and constant worries about insurance, pensions, the washing machine, the residents' association, the children's friends and their progress, global warming, AIDS in Africa, summer holidays, the second home. For them, life in middle age is life on hold: somehow it

will be better in the future. But they also know that time is not on their side. 'We aren't getting any younger, are we?' they say with a wry smile, dishcloth in hand.

5. **Of their time**
If these people know that middle age is happening, they don't show it. They pass seamlessly from youth to old age, and don't make a big fuss about any part of it. Age is unimportant – one is simply the way one feels, and every phase in life has its merits. Youth culture, urban graffiti, cosmetic surgery – they pass no judgement: all are part of the rich mosaic. Life is good, they suggest, and if not, that's life too. But they are fully aware that they've only got one.

TRICKS OF TIME

In middle age, age becomes a serious issue. There are landmark birthdays to be fêted with as much grace as can be mustered. Fifty is usually celebrated with a bit of a fanfare, and with an underlying theme of 'I'm still young'. But with it comes the realisation that at 50, 60 no longer seems so old. At 60 the obvious underlying theme is usually brushed discreetly under the carpet.

It becomes increasingly hard to know how old a person actually is. As you head into middle age, being asked your age isn't appreciated because:

a) you don't like to be reminded;

b) you genuinely cannot remember if you are 48 or 47 without subtracting the year of your birth from the current year – and, what year are we in now?

The bluffer should profess a tolerant attitude to this and feel free to trot out the old clichés that feed the delusion that age is not happening, such as 'You are only as old as you feel.' Leroy 'Satchel' Paige – probably the oldest baseball player ever to appear in a major league game, and author of an autobiography entitled *Maybe I'll Pitch Forever* – revised this truism neatly as a question: 'How old would you be if you didn't know how old you was?'

Alternatively, you can advise middle-agers to take Lucille Ball's approach: 'The secret of staying young is to live honestly, eat slowly, and lie about your age.'

Christmas Again?

Another symptom of middle age is that time seems to accelerate. Years go by faster and faster. It's October when it should still be June. In childhood, time stretched into the infinite future; Christmases were separated by an eternity. Now last year's Christmas tree needles are still lurking in the back of the sofa when it's time to buy a new one.

An analogy for this apparent acceleration of time is useful here. It's as if in life people are walking from the centre towards the outer edge of a giant revolving Busby Berkeley cake. You may walk at a steady pace, but as you move away from the middle, it whirls around beneath your feet at an ever-increasing velocity. Use this image with care, however: you don't want to draw too much attention to what happens when that outer edge is reached.

There is a theory that time accelerates as you get older because each day occupies an increasingly greater proportion of what is left. At the beginning of a soccer match, one minute does not make a lot of difference. At the end, for the players in the team that is one goal down, each declining minute has ever-increasing value and is gone in a flash. They begin to hope for a bit of injury time.

'You pick up speed when you're over the hill,' runs the old adage. But most middle-agers wonder how they can be 'over the hill' when they don't even remember being on top of it. So champion the upside: when time is speeding up, at least there is less likelihood that it will hang heavily. Once a 40-minute physics lesson was an eternity: now it's barely enough time to accomplish anything beyond vacuuming the car, checking a bank statement or plucking some nose-hair.

You Are History

At some point in all middle-agers' trajectory through life will come the sudden, devastating revelation – striking like a bolt from the blue – that one is no longer a part of the happening, current generation.

You now belong to the past; you are becoming archive material. Middle-aged bluffers are wise to make light of this and warn other middle-agers to be prepared for the moments when:

- it dawns on you that you were expecting other (younger) people's baby photos to be in black and white;
- the model of the car you first owned is categorised as a veteran;
- you find yourself unable to communicate measurement to a younger person because he or she doesn't know what an inch is, and you can't think in millimetres;
- you see an old telephone with a dial and realise you are the only one who knows how to use it;
- you catch yourself saying, 'In my day...'

MID-LIFE CRISIS

In middle age, feeling beleaguered on all fronts is a way of life – not all of which is visible. In addition to physical decline, and the sense of a finite life span and mortality, can come general disillusion with the routines that one has so doggedly carved out for oneself. These factors can conspire to produce a profound and disturbing period of self-reassessment, not to mention deep frustration, bloody-mindedness and auto-destruction. It's a phenomenon that goes by the name of 'mid-life crisis'.

The term is usually credited to the London-based psychologist Elliott Jacques, who, in 1965, suggested that the mid-life crisis occurred at the age of 35-40. "Ridiculously young," you will say cheerfully, reminding your audience that at the time of the artists and musicians featured in his study, and indeed the 1960s, everything happened earlier than at present – marriage, children leaving home, cataclysmic mid-life doubt.

Been There, Done That

The mid-life crisis is caused by a shedload of what psychologists call 'negative evaluation' about one's future, one's work and career, relationships, deteriorating health, inability to chill out. A shift has taken place from extrovert youth to the introspection and self-appraisal of middle age, and the outlook does not appear promising.

The crisis may begin with the perception that time is running out, a notion often reinforced by the task of looking after ageing parents, who show what ageing looks like 30 or so years down the line.

Life-threatening illness, or a death in the family's older generation, may also trigger a sharpened sense of mortality and the brevity of life. The average age for experiencing the death of a parent in the West is now about 50.

The middle-aged are still young enough to remember the ambitions, hopes and passions that fuelled their youth, and may still feel young enough to make a last-ditch bid to achieve them. Youth was all about potential, dreams of achievement. Middle age is about coming to terms with reality, which means relinquishing certain expectations; for example, settling for the middle rather than getting to 'the top', or giving up the idea of ever finding anybody who can give you a clear and compelling reason for daylight savings time.

Typically, by middle age you have climbed three-quarters of the way up a second-choice career ladder, but have now come to a halt. Nobody seems to care. Worse, you yourself don't seem to care. It is like the road-to-Damascus moment when the golfer gets three-quarters of the way around the golf-course on a damp afternoon with a new set of painfully expensive clubs, and realises that he or she can't realistically hope to play any better. Or does not in fact really like golf.

In addition, there are factors rarely mentioned at an earlier age, such as:

1. Discrimination

In their work, the middle-aged suddenly realise that they are expendable. Men can suffer from what is known as the 'Old Stag Complex' – they are not quite the stag they once were, and if it comes to a clash of antlers with a younger contender, they are not going to win. Men and women fear that they will lose their job because of age, and it dawns on them that, careerwise, there never was a Plan B. And losing their job, for many people, is the equivalent of losing their identity.

Throughout their youth, they have been promising

themselves that they would achieve great things one day – write a novel, begin an acting career, go into politics, breed pedigree chinchillas, open a museum of biscuit tins. In an earlier decade they were listing famous examples of others who started on such paths late in life. Now they are fast running out of role models. Encourage procrastinating would-be novelists by citing J.R.R. Tolkein, whose first book, *The Hobbit*, was published when he was 45, and Anna Sewell, who entered the ring with *Black Beauty* at the age of 57. Tell them not to leave it until comparisons with Mary Wesley become applicable; her first commercial success, *Camomile Lawn*, occurred when she was 72. 'It's a sobering thought,' said Tom Lehrer, 'that when Mozart was my age he had been dead for two years.'

2. Disillusion

Another symptom of the mid-life crisis is the inability to enjoy leisure time. What middle-agers used to believe would make them happy – company, sex, holidays, football, soft furnishings – no longer delivers. On the social front, they may find it increasingly difficult to make new friends – and fear that they've already got all the friends they are ever going to make. In this state of mind, attending class reunions can be a mistake. Participants may see how much more successful, or just more happy, everyone else has become – even those they once despised. (Also, they feel strangely younger than everyone else looks, until someone sends them the photographs.)

For parents, middle age can coincide with the moment when their hitherto unquestioning offspring become rebellious, resentful, openly critical, and knowing.

The young may also start bringing home girlfriends and boyfriends, to whom the parents feel disturbingly

attracted, and in front of whom they become embar-
rassingly skittish. (Teenage girls learn from an early
age to avoid their father's friends.)

Not only do the parents feel they are becoming an
embarrassment; they no longer feel needed. Deprived
of the distraction of children to occupy their lives and
to act as excuses, the parents have only each other to
focus on for the first time for several decades. The
bluffer may suggest that this offers the couple the
chance to re-find their relationship; but in truth the
'Empty Nest Syndrome' presents both opportunity and
disillusion. This could be the moment when a couple
has to admit that they were never very happy or well
suited. Half of all marriages break down at this time.

Just taking the young to university can be a landmark occasion in middle age. At first it is a puzzle why
so many grandparents are taking their grandchildren
to university. Then the truth dawns: they are not
grandparents at all – but fellow parents.

3. Displacement

A useful term for many of the more surprising
patterns of behaviour among the middle aged is
'displacement'. Psychoanalysts will often say these
are a surrogate – or 'displacement activity' – for something now missing from their lives, such as sex, or
bringing up children, or having a stimulating job or
anything to talk about. For instance, once the house
is empty of children, the parents will often embark on
a massive home-refurbishment programme, adding on
extensions, conservatories, loft conversions – creating
more space when actually less in needed.

Many a middle-aged woman, missing the physical
contact of a husband who has lost interest (or left
home), and the children who have more or less grown

up, acquires a replacement upon which she can lavish attention. Remind your audience of the scene in *Annie Hall* when Woody Allen is being hauled across the road by Annie's dachshund and she admits that for her, it's not so much a dog as a 'penis substitute'.

4. Becoming Invisible

It is important to acknowledge that men and women experience the mid-life crisis in entirely different ways. For men it is often a question of the faltering career, loss of direction and the decline in sexual magnetism and performance. With women it's about physical deterioration, fear of becoming unattractive to one's partner, and separation from children as they move on. Also, significantly, being taken for granted and under-appreciated, especially by offspring who, happy to use the hotel facilities of home, have turned into boomerangs and keep coming back.

A common feeling for both men and women in social contexts is that, overnight, they have become invisible. They used to feel noticed, attractive to the opposite sex, and enjoyed some flirtatious glances and banter. They felt desired, even if they weren't going to do much about it. Now they walk into a room and no-one notices. The modern world prefers youth.

A key concept to latch on to here is approval – or rather the loss of it. In youth, approval by others is one of the main contributors to the sense of self-worth. In middle age this kind of affirmation becomes increasingly hard to win. Be kind. Rejection and lack of regard are more difficult to take in middle life. When you are younger you bounce back. In middle age bouncing can seem like far too much effort.

All such tribulations might be smoothed away if the afflicted middle-ager pursued some new interests and directions. But physical decline is also kicking in. The middle-aged feel increasingly fatigued. The very thought of going to a jazz club is exhausting because the main sets won't begin until 2 a.m., and it will be difficult getting home.

Sex, More or Less

When the menopause and the menoporsche come to haunt a household, the results in the bedroom can be complex. The loss of hormones can devastate the libido on both sides of the marriage bed. The mind may still be active, stimulated by sex-saturated advertising and re-runs of *Sex in the City,* but the flesh is not always willing. Bed is increasingly a place for sleep – or it would be, were it not for the snoring.

Men become increasingly difficult to get to bed at all: they fall asleep on the sofa during the ten o'clock news. Where once they had come-to-bed eyes, now they have gone-to-bed eyes. Many a wife has a need to explain that her spouse's going to sleep at the dinner table is not a comment on the company.

Men tend to blame women for a loss in sexual appetite. Women blame men for having too much. Some surveys suggest that as many as 80% of women would rather have a good meal than sex. (Some qualify this by saying that this refers only to having sex with their husband.) But according to other sex surveys (always good waters for the bluffer to fish in) at least 50% of men and women over 70 are sexually active – and that can't be just the men. You could argue that it is incumbent upon middle-agers to rise to this challenge. In a French survey, 93% of men and women aged 45 said they were happy with their sex lives. (In France, you should add archly, it is possible to have sex and a good meal.)

However, if your sex life or that of your audience is good, you can claim that regular sex has been statistically shown to make people not only live longer, but look younger for longer as well. It gets the heart pumping faster; it also pumps up the release of muscle-promoting human-growth hormones. On the other hand, if you or your listener is not getting enough, you can stand by the rumour that every orgasm is reputed to shorten your life.

With the reduction in hormones that accompanies middle age, it is to be expected that the sex drive should diminish. But in all stages of life, the sex drive is virtually an autonomous state – a rogue state armed with weapons of mass destruction. A feature of middle age is sexual misbehaviour, perpetrated by both genders. Where hormones can't be held responsible, blame may fall on fears and insecurities. The middle-aged fear that their youthful vigour and good looks are on the wane. An affair provides the reassurance that they are still attractive.

A new merger with someone much younger can look good statistically: the average age of a couple can be slashed at a stroke. As some would say: 'You are only as old as the thing you squeeze.'

Of course, the average age can be reduced even more dramatically with a stroke of the other kind. The excitement of extra-marital affairs can be literally fatal. Reports show that:

a) a man's heartbeat rises to 130 beats per minute during illicit sex (compared to 100 when with his wife);

b) 80% of male heart-attacks that occur during love-making take place when the man is not with his wife.

Bluffers may legitimately ponder aloud about quite how such facts were researched, but will never let doubt get in the way of a valuable statistic.

Spotting the Crisis

A mid-life crisis is easy to spot not so much through its symptoms as through the responses to them. These can take a number of forms that may, on the surface, look perfectly innocent. They include:

– moving house;
– moving country;
– joining a religion;
– taking up amateur dramatics/skydiving/marathon running/gambling;
– having an affair, divorcing and following the big snake all the way down to Square One with a new spouse, hostile step-children and a clutch of new babies;
– abandoning a career to work for a charity;
– going clubbing like there is no tomorrow (which may turn out to be the case);
– having a complete mental breakdown;
– attempting to row across the Atlantic in a skiff.

The result can be tragic: wrecked marriages, traumatised families, ruined careers, disastrous new relationships, a boat at the bottom of the ocean.

Bluffers will need to be at the pinnacle of their art here. It is helpful to anyone going through a mid-life trauma to suggest that all crises have a constructive, creative function. You can suggest that middle age is, rightfully, a time to stand back, reassess and refocus.

This argument may not always be quite as hopeless as it sounds. Middle age is often accompanied by greater stability in relationships, self-confidence, self-knowledge and the satisfying sense of experience. So if they are still a priority, long-cherished goals and dreams may now indeed be feasible and accessible for the first time – through the very circumstances that middle age can provide.

On the other hand, such encouragement may prove fatally unnerving: it was easier to contemplate those dreams when they weren't accessible, staring at one's toes poking through the bubble bath.

GETTING PSYCHED UP

There is a body of psychological research on which you can draw for your bluffing. Those responsible have, in the self-defeating way of experts everywhere, labelled it 'developmental psychology'. To prevent your audience falling asleep before you've even started (always a danger with the middle-aged, of course), it could be advisable to change this title to something that will have greater resonance for them. The 'psychology of the Jung at Heart', perhaps.

A number of fertile brains have been at this topic and have divided the development through life into a series of stages. These are the most useful:

Erik Erikson

Psychoanalyst Erik Erikson is known as the 'father of adult development'. In the 1950s he identified eight 'psycho-social' stages from childhood to old age, three of which covered adulthood. Each of these stages, he proposed, is accompanied by a crisis, which permits the individual to move on to the next stage. As a result of successful progression, the individual can achieve a sense of self-fulfilment, or 'ego integrity'. Stage 7 is 'Middle Adulthood' (age 40-65), with the crisis 'Generativity versus Stagnation' (generativity meaning the ability to think of others, and to build some kind of

40

legacy by which one's life will be remembered).

One point is worth noting. Erikson believed that a crisis did not mean the sort of meltdown usually implied by the term 'mid-life crisis', but a turning point. This is more in tune with the original meaning of crisis, from the Greek *krinein*, meaning to decide. Caution middle-agers against using this linguistic nicety as an excuse. If a woman discovers her husband in bed with his 18-year-old secretary, what he is facing is most definitely a crisis.

Abraham Maslow

American psychologist Maslow identified four stages of life; by satisfactory completion of the fourth, one can achieve 'self-actualisation'. It's a buzzword that speaks for itself.

Sigmund Freud

The 'father of psychoanalysis', Freud divided human life into childhood and adulthood. This can be used as powerful testimony to the view that mid-life does not exist at all.

Carl Jung

Jung had a mid-life crisis of his own aged 38-44 (as a result of which he fell out with Freud). This event led to the first proper analysis of the personality changes that take place in the second half of life. He wasn't exactly complimentary, seeing mid-life as a watershed to maturity which necessarily involves some kind of crisis. With Jung, the quest was always to achieve a sense of identity by means of the passage through life's experiences. He signalled five steps in this process. Essentially, mid-life is seen as the period when the personae, or characteristics, adopted in youth to accommodate the outside world have to be addressed and transformed to find one's true self. The gap between the personae of youth and one's true self is an indicator of the size of crisis that will have to be endured to find a resolution. This usually involves a conflict between extrovert and introvert tendencies, and is often resolved through unconscious forces rather than rational thought. For some in your audience, the idea of rational thought being absent in middle age will ring only too true.

Mid-life also coincides with the awakening of a man's anima (the feminine psychological tendency, previously repressed) and the woman's equivalent, the animus. A certain amount of time may be spent in psychological no man's land before the harmonious integration of the conscious and unconscious aspects of personality can be achieved – what Jung called 'individuation', and what in an ordinary household is called 'peace at last'.

Daniel J. Levinson

Professor of Psychology at Yale University, Levinson first came to prominence in the 1970s, ultimately producing *The Seasons of a Man's Life*. He called the stage from the mid-40s to the early 60s the 'mid-life transition'. He placed the mid-life crisis slightly later than Elliott Jacques (who suggested the age-band of 35-40) but was in no doubt about its prevalence: 80% of men told him that they had gone through a personal crisis at this time. Levinson suggested that the remaining 20% were simply in denial.

The French

The French do not have a word for middle age at all. A person is of 'a certain age' or *entre deux âges* (between two ages), and thus gratifyingly lumped in with students, sports stars, catwalk models and newly weds. The French have no problem in associating age with beauty. The sexual allure of a Jeanne Moreau or a Catherine Deneuve does not diminish as time goes by. *Au contraire*, to the fertile mind of a Frenchman it increases: imagine everything she'll have learned.

Someone might argue that, just because there isn't a word for it, does not mean that this age-phase does not exist; but you can parry this by pointing out that the French do not have a word for 'lap' either, but they still know where to put their portable computers and erotic dancers.

The Bluffer

The flippant may prefer this version of the Three Ages of Man:

1) Childhood;
2) Youth;
3) 'You're looking well.'

Crisis? What Crisis?

Some psychologists argue that there is no such thing as the mid-life crisis at all. Their reasoning is that the symptoms of the alleged crisis are comparable to any other kind of crisis that can occur at any age, so the only distinguishing feature is the age-band implicit in the term. In other words it is a label in search of a phenomenon.

One theory about people in the Western world is that of the 'social clock'. Culturally they are brought up with a certain, fairly fixed notion of the stages of life: they begin work in their 20s, marry and raise a family in their 20s/30s/40s, retire in their 60s. The crisis is programmed into the social clock in the mid-life period. Research in China suggests that this is not an accepted part of their culture. There the word for crisis is made up of two characters, one meaning 'danger', and the other 'opportunity'. It seems the Chinese don't make a drama out of a crisis.

In the West, concerns about one's identity, the physical changes to one's body, the sense of loss as one gets older, and separation from loved ones – are all symptoms of adolescence, just as much as of middle age. This may explain why some middle-agers behave like adolescents, especially when exposed to their company. Adolescents remind the middle-aged of another part of themselves that may have been long buried.

Statistics from the 1980s show as many as 70-80% of the middle-aged had experienced some kind of mid-life crisis; by the early 1990s this figure had dropped to 50%. A recent survey in the U.S. suggested that, whereas 90% of respondents had a clear idea of what a mid-life crisis is, only 25% said they had experienced such a thing. The responses of men and women were remarkably similar, and not one woman who claimed to have had a crisis mentioned the menopause. Contrary to expectations, the majority suggested that in mid-life they had never been happier.

Even those who had experienced a crisis identified the cause as some traumatic unexpected event, such as a brush with serious illness, redundancy or bereavement. This is a useful survey to keep in stock should you need to silence middle-agers who excessively bemoan their mid-life 'crisis'. Mention of heart attacks and funerals will ensure a swift end to complaints about their 36-inch waist.

Refer to the academic Arnold Kruger, who labelled the mid-life crisis 'an unreal creature of the imagination'. Then add: 'Yes, so's Dracula, but he still scares us rigid.'

USE IT OR LOSE IT

The middle-aged are only too aware that time is slipping by. Not only do they have a sharpened sense of mortality; they also have an accompanying concern about their impending old age. They are reminded incessantly about it – by the government, by insurance companies, by their doctors – and implored to plan for it. But in planning meticulously for old age, many people run the risk of allowing middle age to pass them by. Doris Day expressed this fear when she said, 'The really frightening thing about middle age is the knowledge that you'll grow out of it.'

A good name to mention here is Walter B. Pitkin, an American psychologist who in 1934 published the book *Life Begins at Forty* that became so popular, a Hollywood movie based on it appeared the following year. Positive Thinking is a well-known stimulant for staying young. As Thomas Arnold said: 'Probably the happiest period in life most frequently is in middle age, when the eager passions of youth are cooled, and the infirmities of age not yet begun; as we see that the shadows, which are at morning and evening so large, almost entirely disappear at midday.'

If anyone smirks, fall back on Maurice Chevalier's salutory message: 'Age is not so hard when you consider the alternative.'

Body Maintenance

A key difference between youth and middle age is that in middle age the body simply won't take care of itself any more. It requires work.

While the bluffers need to acknowledge this, it is helpful to point out that there is a conspiracy to make the middle-aged feel inadequate. The government issues edicts about obesity, doctors suck their teeth when reading the sphygmomanometer, and cosmetic companies relentlessly suggest that anyone could fight off age by passing money in their direction. Pressures like this tend to dictate the choice of action when it comes to body maintenance. There are three main options: complete refit, respray, and regular servicing.

Complete Refit

The 16th-century Spanish conquistador Juan Ponce de León scoured the Caribbean Sea for the fabled island of the Fountain of Youth, and thought he had found it. Today so many aged Americans flock there that, in its public image, youth is not exactly the first word that springs to mind. It's called Florida.

The point to make here is that even if they do not find the Fountain of Youth exactly, at least they can create a convincing illusion of having done so. Virtual eternal youth is now available from the good doctors by way of cosmetic surgery – facelifts and 'peels', stomach and thigh tucks, liposuction, Botox injections, breast enlargement, chin-lifting, collagen and silicone implants, laser treatment (for zapping those liver spots and facial 'resurfacing').

Fortunately, only a scintilla of knowledge about the detail is required here, because as soon as you begin describing the procedures your listeners will turn green and change the subject. A superficial understanding of Botox will suffice.

Botox is the muscle-paralysing bacteria botulinum, a toxin that also moonlights as the cause of the lethal food-poisoning called botulism, and as a chemical weapon. Botox injections flatten out wrinkles (for about four months) by relaxing and paralysing the muscles. Applied to the forehead and around the eyes, it can eliminate surprise from the roll-call of facial expressions, which is why, if a woman follows her friends down this path, none of them look a bit surprised that she also chooses to do so. In fact, the only person left looking surprised is the person who gets the bill.

The burgeoning cosmetic surgery industry is always keen to point out that increasing numbers of men are now indulging in little nips and tucks to keep themselves spry. Italian surgeons were rubbing their hands with glee when the male uptake for cosmetic surgery leaped 30% after prime minister Silvio Berlusconi went under the knife to eliminate droopiness around the eyes (blepharoplasty). But the vast majority of patients (80% in the U.S.) are of course women. The American gospel singer Cora Harvey Armstrong may help to explain this with her quip: 'Inside every older woman is a young girl wondering what the hell happened.'

Such quick-fix solutions can keep a woman looking permanently young, and after a few visits – because she is now incapable of any other expression – looking permanently happy. This is useful, because it is movement that ages skin. A female who wants to stay looking younger for longer is best advised not to adopt any facial expression at all.

However, you ought to be aware that with cosmetic surgery the bottom line is the effect it produces. And the most important effect experienced by just about all participants is that they feel that they look younger. And if they look younger, they feel younger in every way.

All forms of cosmetic treatment entail a certain element of risk. The side effects of Botox treatment include headaches, scarring, bleeding, numbness and paralysis. But there is no truth in the rumour that after successive facelifts a woman may end up with her navel becoming the dimple on her chin.

Respray

The next step down from the operating table is the beauty salon. Here the main focus is on the face ('facials'), but all self-respecting salons will offer an extensive menu that includes such things as detox, electronic waves, exfoliation, manual lymphatic massage, micro-currents, and sunbeds and seaweed wraps. 'Guns' armed with needles deliver hyaluronic acid (produced by fibroblasts) to stimulate moisture retention; pressure jets are used to fire out streams of pure oxygen. Effective treatments cost an arm and a leg, hence Joan Collins' comment when asked how she kept looking so young: 'All it takes is money, darling.'

A cheaper alternative is 'non invasive skin care', i.e., age-beating creams or lotions. Advertisements for these are illustrated by models who (miraculously) have not a wrinkle on them, and come replete with the kind of quasi-science that the bluffer appreciates. Super-active terms like co-enzymes, amino-peptides, nanosomes, retinol (a fancy name for Vitamin A) are tossed about with more comforting, healthy-sounding natural products such as apple seed, papaya and pomegranate. It's the modern version of the witches scene in *Macbeth*.

You can go either of two ways with this:

1. Back the ingredients for all you're worth (probably wise since many middle-agers will have used, or be planning to use, or have a mistress who is using, at least one of these sorts of cream). Mention the mystical powers attached to plants that suggest longevity, such as the 'immortelle' flower from France, which never wilts and withers – and nor, by implication, do users of creams made from its extract. Those to whom this line of reasoning appeals might also go for ointments made from the extract of the long-living ginkgo biloba tree of pre-historic origins. Its users, naturally, should not take it personally that it is also known as the fossil or dinosaur tree.

2. Question the manufacturers' logic. Some lotions, for instance, contain royal jelly, which is what keeps the Queen Bee alive 40 times longer than the workers. "That's not what keeps her young," you intone. "What keeps her young is the fact that everyone else is doing all the work."

No stone is left unturned in the quest for rejuvenation. An old favourite is cod-liver oil, a catch-all remedy for just about every ill that visits the middle-aged from the onset of memory loss, to creaky knees. One new discovery (also made from fish) is the beneficial antioxidant effects of the alcohol DMAE – dimethylaminoethanol – a splendid term to commit to mind. It is so good at smoothing, plumping and lifting – all excellent verbs to toy with in this context – that there barely seems to be any need to go to the gym.

Sea-anemones also need to look out: it has been revealed that they show no sign of ageing at all. Within no time, the men in white coats will be lining the shores waiting for the tide to go out.

Manufacturers of all beauty products work on the well-tested commercial principle that the more you spend the better you will feel (and in middle age, feeling better means feeling younger). The smaller the pot, the more precious the contents seem; and the smaller the pot, the smaller the print. In fact, for the average middle-aged consumer, the print is practically invisible, and she can't remember where she put the pot anyway.

Regular Servicing

Some people prefer not to turn to medicine and the pharmaceutical industry for help, but choose to do battle with middle age through a more proactive approach – by means of diet and physical exercise. Both have their pitfalls, so it behoves you to advocate the benefits, even if you are entirely in sympathy with the person who said: 'I don't exercise, it makes the ice jump right out of my glass.'

Getting Physical

It is scientifically acknowledged that physically fit people look 15 to 20 years younger than their calendar age. Pumping the body's system through exercise helps to burn fat, strengthens the bones, pushes blood to the brain, circulates the sugars needed for cell growth, promotes the natural production of antioxidants, and recycles waste. In fact, moderate exercise seems to induce many of the advantages that medical scientists seek. (This is, of course, highly subversive information which could wreck a whole industry, so bluffers should use it with discretion.)

A handy term is 'muscle mass', although it is increasingly used in the negative in middle age, as men develop their chicken legs, and women their droopy upper arms known as 'bingo wings', as revealed when raising an arm to proclaim 'bingo!'

Exercise, it needs to be said, again and again, improves muscle mass. Yet it is difficult for middle-agers to take up exercise without implying that this is a latter-day rescue bid to combat middle age (which of course it is). A sudden change to physical exertion after years of pasture can be fatal, so newcomers have to be content with moving in a low gear to start with.

They also should be alerted to the danger of 'impact'. Ageing joints are particularly vulnerable to impact, and so it may be necessary to bin the semi-perished gym-shoes that have spent a lifetime awaiting rediscovery beneath the wooden racket-press and, however ridiculous they may look to the mature eye, purchase a new pair of high-tech trainers with good 'impact absorption'. Then master the technique of making it look as though you are among the 3% who have been taking exercise all along.

Dieting

All middle-aged people will be on a diet at some stage, especially those who incline towards Phyllis Diller's declaration: 'My idea of exercise is a good brisk sit.'

Bluffers will therefore enquire at any encounter: 'Have you lost weight?' in an admiring tone, even if all evidence is to the contrary. The fact is that in middle age you should eat less because you need about 10% fewer calories than you did when you were in your twenties. But middle-agers tend not to eat less and they don't burn off the calories – which happily scurry off down the digestive tract and take up residence as fat.

Diets can take a wide variety of forms, but these are the four main categories:

1. **Put your money where your mouth is**
The more someone spends on the diet – manuals, special foods, slimming clubs, electrical equipment – the greater is the conviction that it will succeed.

2. **Suffer for it**
The dieter invests all hope and faith in one particular food or product, such as grapefruit, cabbage soup, lemonade, or rice cakes that taste like polystyrene foam. It is quite important that this chosen foodstuff is unpalatable or even repulsive, as this will increase the notion of martyrdom that is essential to the experience, and which no-one is allowed to ignore.

3. **One rule solves all**
All dieters need to do is cut out one element in their diet – carbohydrates (as in the Atkins diet), red meat, animal fat, bread, beer, potatoes, chocolate – and then they are free to gorge themselves to their heart's content on anything that takes their fancy. It seems also essential for the rosy-cheeked adherents to proselytise incessantly until even they can tell this strategy has made no difference at all, and the obvious failure of the scheme becomes an embarrassment.

4. **My doctor says**
Basically, the doctor says: 'If it tastes good, you can't eat it.' Unlike the other three methods, the cachet of a medical warning protects the dieter from dismissive ribbing by friends and colleagues, and so helps elevate the notion of martyrdom towards sainthood.

All bluffers know, of course, that the sensible way to lose weight in middle age is simply to eat less and exercise more. But they also know that no-one is interested in this. It has the same style-failure of commonsense, and there's no money in it. Therefore

you need to have a few sensible, low-cost suggestions
to make, that won't harm anyone. (They will of course
be ignored – but at least it shows you've tried.)

Low fat/high fruit and veg
The fruit and vegetables are plum-full of antioxidants
lining up to do battle with those pesky free radicals.
Low fat means low in calories, and low calories mean
longer life – according to laboratory tests on mice.
Reduce a mouse's calorie intake by 60% and it lives 50%
longer. (But reduce it by 100% and it lives 0% longer.)

Hunza apricots
The people of the Hunza region of northern Pakistan
all live to about 180. Those wishing to follow suit may
not be able to emulate their high altitude, sun-filled
valleys and annual income of $500, but they can eat
Hunza sun-dried apricots.

The Mediterranean diet
Everyone knows that the people of the Mediterranean
live longer but rarely look older than 37. This is
because they drink mono-unsaturated-fat-rich olive
oil, and eat loads of fresh fruit and vegetables, and
have never heard of ice-cream, moussaka, pasta,
pizza, zabaglione or tiramisù.

Red wine
This contains the antioxidant resveratrol, which
attacks free radicals and can help to reduce heart
disease and cancer. It is also a word that becomes
impossible to say if you have had too much, so get it
out before you start.

Blueberries or bilberries
Geriatric rats fed with supplements of these berries
have been found to have better motor and learning

skills than those that were not, and could outperform them when balancing on a rod. This could be useful to middle-agers planning to take up gymnastics, or simply propping up the bar.

Sardines
Fish contain a youth-inducing nucleic acid (DNA and RNA). The claims for sardines can be bulked up by mentioning the wrinkle-busting antioxidant DMAE. Then throw in the Omega-3 factor – fatty acids that help reduce high blood pressure, and the risk of heart disease, strokes and Alzheimer's – and sardines make an irrefutable case. Some dieticians recommend eating a can of sardines four times a week. They have the further advantages of being cheap, and no-one is going to come too close to argue.

Water
That dried-up look is what it says: dehydrated body cells. Water comes out of the tap without any small-print, and – for the eco-conscious – is eminently recyclable. Some middle-agers think that alcohol in prodigious quantities has the same effect, but they are confusing rehydration with pickling.

Sleep

This is one of the most effective and least expensive of all anti-ageing treatments. Bluffers know that lack of sleep produces cavernous or puffy eyes, sallow skin, haystack hair and the hangdog look. But, as ever, you should recruit a bit of the science to argue your case whenever the opportunity arises. Fatigue disrupts 'cell turnover': it's in bed with those damaging free radicals. The ageing body needs rest and recuperation, and some bodies – on the sofa in front of the television, or after a very liquid lunch – can be in unseemly haste to get started.

It is better not to refer to the many who simply can't sleep, because of job worries, general irritability, the menopause, strategic avoidance of their spouse, snoring – in fact, a host of reasons, all of which are associated with middle age.

Ageing Gracefully

All counteractive measures designed to combat ageing – dieting, exercise, renovation, restoration, subterfuge – require work, thought, energy and low lighting. The conscientious middle-ager has to be trainer, dietician, beautician, motivator and drill-sergeant all in one, from the moment that each day breaks. Fighting age can make some people miserable. It's enough to make you age.

Surveys looking into what makes older people look and feel younger have revealed a whole range of things such as optimism, an interest in novelty and challenge, being curious, a sense of humour, and a really good mattress. They have also shown that stress is a major cause of ageing, and that those who have strategies – either intuitive or learned – for keeping stress at bay often look and feel younger. Clearly, this is not easy to prescribe; and even thinking about it may cause stress.

The concept of 'ageing gracefully' implies a lack of stress. Why go to all the effort of fighting age if you can drift elegantly towards your dotage, and win admirers for the casual insouciance of your approach? There is a beauty in wrinkles: they are the physical expression of experience, character, and a life well lived.

Bluffers should adopt the pretence of being entirely content to go along with this idea. They know that, behind the scenes, those said to be 'ageing gracefully' are very likely to be making strenuous efforts to slow the decline. The difference is that they also make equally strenuous efforts to conceal the signs of battle. Those who believe they can age gracefully without effort run the risk of embracing Ageing Gracefully's less attractive counterpart: 'Letting Yourself Go'.

Medicine to the Rescue

Science may be able to put names to what is happening in the ageing process, but as yet the reasons why time affects the body remain a profound mystery. But before many years have passed, science will probably have come to the rescue by tackling and modifying the root causes. The three main culprits are: cells, hormones and genes. If the damage done to these by ageing could be halted or even reversed, then ageing could be treated like a cold that needs curing.

Too late, of course, for the middle-agers you are busily bluffing. But console them with the words of Jean-Paul Sartre: 'The more sand has escaped from the hourglass of our life, the clearer we should see through it.' (Be careful, however, not to lay any stress on the word 'should'.)

Cells

In the long term, it should be possible to tailor new and healthy body parts in the laboratory by using human cells as building blocks. This kind of 'tissue engineering' is already being used to produce bone, skin and cartilage. The use of stem cells – which form after conception and hold the formula for all body part cells – promises to accelerate this development. Soon whole organs could be farmed, which could then be fitted as easily as a new exhaust pipe. Prepare middle-agers for surgeons charging three times their original estimate, saying, "It's not the parts, see, it's the labour."

Hormones

Success with hormones may be closer at hand. Scientists are looking at a number of hormones connected to the ageing process. Melatonin is being targeted. It is produced by the pineal gland in the brain, and – it is scientifically acceptable to be vague here – it seems to have an influence in the way the body's biological clock functions. Another good one is DHEA. Quite what it does is largely unknown, but quantities of DHEA in the body decline with advancing age, so if the process is reversible benefits may follow. Also, its full name – dehydroepiandrosterone – may be useful to trump the opposition in a pub quiz.

The most promising is the growth hormone (GH), secreted by the pituitary gland. This activity declines with age – a process known as somatopause (from the Greek *soma*, 'body', and *pausis*, 'halt'). The result is a loss of lean body mass, and a growth of body fat. In other words, the middle age spread.

What is not known is whether somatopause serves as a safety net in the process of ageing, or if GH replacement by injection or supplements (already commercially available) could halt ageing. Should your listener start rolling up a shirtsleeve there and then, tell them it's unnecessary; GH production is stimulated naturally by sleep and exercise, so normal exercise routines could be equally effective, especially if performed in bed.

Genes

Longevity, and the preservation of good health and good looks into old age, to some extent depend on genetic inheritance, so genetic modification (GM) may hold some promise. Middle-aged GM crop protesters have been known to change their tune when the promise of a perfect shape and complexion is made to them rather than the apricot.

Some genes, for example APOE4 (apolipoprotein E4) have been directly linked to higher occurrence of certain ageing problems, like coronary heart disease. However, at present only about 25% of ageing can be blamed on genes. Most of the remainder of the pie-chart is occupied by big slices of diet, exercise, living conditions, and paranoia about maintenance payments.

The measly 25% genetic inheritance factor may, however, come in very handy when reassuring someone whose father keeled over at the age of 54, or whose mother has become a desiccated prune, and 'difficult' with it.

The Time of Your Life

In fact, the ages of about 45 to 65 can be some of the best years of anyone's life. Bluffers can happily wheel out Carl Jung to support this theory: 'The greatest potential for growth and self-realisation exists in the second half of life.'

By middle age most people are self-confident enough to know what they want and to take risks. Their children have become more independent. So, provided they can shake off the conditioning of decades of routine and self-denial, middle-agers are able to indulge. "Take full advantage," the bluffer should declare: "You've paid the price – getting older."

With a following wind, middle age can be portrayed as a time of liberation. The American historian and poet Hervey Allen stated: 'The young are slaves to dreams; the old [are] servants of regrets.' That, you can say, leaves middle age in clover, spanning the two.

Middle age is the time to actively pursue dreams never realised. It's an inspiring fact that on an expedition to Mount Kilimanjaro which had an average age of 50, only the three youngest ones (19, 24 and 37) failed. Altitude sickness often affects younger people the most. So encourage middle-agers to get the easel out of the attic, do a degree, plant a vineyard, or start their own dating parties for the 'Unaccountably Single'.

Wealth is not essential – in fact, wealth can be an impediment, giving access to too broad a choice. The one factor that may be in short supply is time. Therefore, the middle-aged have to be persuaded to prioritise, focus on what they do best, and cut out what they don't want, or need, to do. 'At forty-six,' wrote Virginia Woolf, 'one must be a miser; only have time for essentials.'

Playing the Long Game

Middle age can bring a sense of ease, as well as a renewed wonderment about the ordinary things in life – things that in youth one had taken for granted. The twist in the petals of a red cyclamen can now stir the heart as much as the glint on the bonnet of a Ferrari once did.

But the middle-aged should not be encouraged to slow down too much. It appears from modern neurological research that the brain behaves a bit like a muscle, and needs regular exercise to keep it trim. So suggest 'cognitively stimulating activities' such as crossword puzzles, Spanish classes, researching a method of opening milk cartons without soaking oneself.

Above all, prevail upon the anxious middle-ager not to panic. Trying to mask age tends to draw attention to the mask. Panic can produce regrettable results. The vocabulary for those that err is unforgiving: the trophy wife, the ageing Lothario, mutton dressed as lamb, and – most hurtful of all – 'wonderful for your age'.

It's enough to determine many to age disgracefully – to head towards old age in a blaze of fireworks. These are the ones who see middle age as an opportunity to throw caution to the wind, to go rock-climbing, paint the garage door like a Jackson Pollock, wear a T-shirt to a wedding. Such reprobates will talk to complete strangers, say what they like to whomever they please. They buy that Hawaiian shirt, the leather jacket they craved in their youth, the bright red dress and the Manolo Blahniks. Clearly they are all believers in the George Burns school of thought: 'You can't help getting older, but you don't have to get old.'

Middle age, you can tell anyone listening, is a marathon not a sprint. The trick is to adjust one's goals and make sure they are always obtainable.

So perhaps the best strategy to advocate in middle age is to:

1. set targets low,
2. adopt a gentle pace, and
3. plan to go the distance.

THINGS TO KNOW ABOUT MIDDLE AGE

You grunt involuntarily as you bend down.

You sigh as you sit down.

If you raise yourself from the vegetable compartment of the fridge in one, unaided push-up from the knees, you feel really smug about it.

You talk back at the TV or radio.

You take your garden furniture to a picnic.

You are no longer repulsed by the details of other people's operations.

You discover that your favourite rock anthem has been muzacked.

You think it makes good sense to dress according to the weather.

A trip to the supermarket demands the precision planning of a military manoeuvre.

You start to keep empty Benecol tubs because you never know when they will come in handy.

When faced with a choice between two appealing things to do in an evening, you choose the one that will get you home earlier.

Omar Sharif, Bryan Ferry, Helen Mirren and Tina Turner don't look that old to you.

GLOSSARY

AAADD (Age Activated Attention Deficit Disorder) – the phenomenon that means you get distracted before the end of 'Age Activated Attention Deficit Disorder'.

ageing – an issue of mind over matter. If you don't mind, it doesn't matter.

arm candy – the young object of affection of a sugar daddy or sugar mummy.

augmentation – surgical term for a breast enhancement involving rather more than titivation.

body mass index (BMI) – fancy expression for weight that makes it seem less offensive, as in 'normal BMI' and 'higher BMI' (i.e., overweight). The abbreviation sounds faintly medical, which always pleases the hypochondriac.

climacteric – another word for menopause, not widely adopted because it sounds so wholly inappropriate.

denture venturers – the mature adult (or post-larval) stage of the back-packer.

DUMPIES – Desperately Unprepared Mature People.

exercise – what needs to be done early in the morning before your brain figures out what you're doing.

expression lines – the trade name for wrinkles when their elimination is not a priority. They can be lovingly preserved with expensive ointments.

grey power – authority that comes when you no longer view issues as quite so black and white.

lived-in look – the look that lives in between racy and raddled.

memory loss – when your secrets are safe with your friends because they can't remember them either.

middle age – a) the age that begins five years after your next birthday; b) when ads for small hair clippers take on a new significance.

mid-life crisis – optimistic term that assumes the sufferers are going to survive to live the other half.

mid-lifer – U.S. term for middle-ager, avoided by the British for the unfortunate suggestion of a prison sentence, without remission.

MOSS – Middle-aged, Overstressed, Semi-affluent Suburbanites: the reverse-side of yuppiedom.

saturated fats – a) delicious food fats that go solid when cool (cheese, butter, lard, dripping), and when ingested readily convert into body fat, cholesterol and every other life-threatening evil that haunts the middle-aged; b) those who watch TV on a Saturday afternoon from a horizontal position.

self-deception – necessary bullet-proof vest against inexorable decline.

STML (Short Term Memory Loss) – reason why the middle-aged frequently forget to act their age.

trout pout – lips that broadcast the fact that the wearer has swallowed the beauty consultant's advice hook, line and sinker.

rejuvenation – middle-agers' quest that represents the victory of hope over experience.

rhytidectomy – the fancy word for a facelift (from the Greek for wrinkle); the more you have, the more ridiculously difficult the word gets to pronounce. Too many and, if you want to smile, you may need to cross your legs to give yourself some slack.

THE AUTHOR

Antony Mason is a mere 50 years old, so really in the first bloom of middle age. He is determined not to be alarmed by his failing sight, or the fact that his yellowing teeth seem to be migrating towards the back of his head, and that his hair – after going absent without leave several decades ago – has now decided to re-emerge from his nose and ears.

None of this bothers him, because he thinks he is still 18 (oh all right then, 28). He is the author of *The Bluffer's Guide to Men*, and about 60 books on anything from pot plants to volleyball. Given that hopeless optimism is an essential qualification of his profession, he is still full of ambition and willing to try anything that stems the tide of advancing age, such as avoiding full-length mirrors and taking regular exercise with a cocktail shaker. He is currently giving serious thought to the advice received on a card: Happy Birthday... Abandon health foods – in middle age you need all the preservatives you can get.

Further titles in the Bluffer's® Guide series:

Accountancy, Archaeology, Astrology & Fortune Telling, Ballet, Chess, The Classics, Computers, Consultancy, Cricket, Doctoring, Economics, The Flight Deck, Football, Golf, The Internet, Jazz, Law, Management, Marketing, Men, Men & Women, Music, Opera, Philosophy, Public Speaking, The Quantum Universe, Relationships, The Rock Business, Rugby, Science, Secretaries, Seduction, Sex, Skiing, Small Business, Stocks & Shares, Tax, Teaching, University, Whisky, Wine, Women.

www.bluffers.com